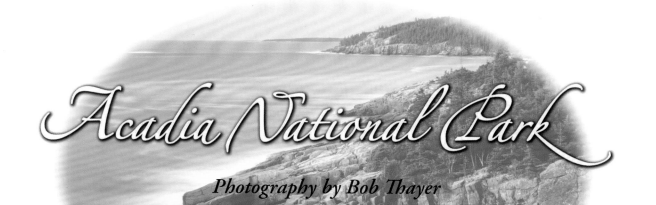

Acadia National Park

Photography by Bob Thayer

Acadia National Park

Photographer – Bob Thayer

ISBN: 978-1-60068-557-6

First Printing, April 2013

Proudly Designed & Distributed in the U.S.A.
www.impactphotographics.com
© IMPACT PHOTOGRAPHICS

The ocean may be Acadia's greatest attraction, but from its mountain vistas to its wooded carriage roads Acadia National Park houses the best of what the coast of Maine has to offer.

From the summit of Cadillac Mountain can be seen the first rays of the rising sun, a perfect way to start a visit to Acadia National Park.

The Park Loop Road is one the most scenic byways in Maine. Its 20 miles circle the eastern half of Mount Desert Island, with another 3.5 mile road going to the summit of Cadillac Mountain.

Somes Sound divides the island nearly in half. The ocean runs 5 miles into the center of the island filling this glacially carved valley.

The group of islands off the coast of Bar Harbor are called the Porcupines because of their humped shapes and the sharp quills of spruce trees that cover them.

Sand Beach is an anomaly along Maine's rocky coast. Deposited by the surf into Newport Cove, the "sand" is actually half sand and half shell pieces.

The peninsula on the far end of Sand Beach is Great Head, rising 145 feet from the ocean. This is the highest headland on the Atlantic coast of the United States.

The sea eats away at the shore leaving us with monuments of granite and beaches of smooth rounded cobblestones.

Thunder Hole is a must stop for any visit to Acadia. The best time to see Thunder Hole is about two hours before high tide or whenever an ocean storm brings high surf to the coast.

Boats of every size and shape use the waters around Acadia.
Deep harbors, beautiful scenery and a sea floor rich with
lobsters create seasonal but dependable industries.

Fog is the result when moist air meets the cool ocean. It often lingers over the islands which are cooler than the surrounding waters.

The moon is a driving force in creating the tides. Acadia's tidal range generally varies between 8 to 14 feet depending on the phase of the moon.

Tide pools are dynamic environments with a twice daily flood of cold sea water. These intertidal areas are surprisingly rich in plant and animal life, such as sea urchins and sea stars.

In 1604, Acadia's treeless mountain summits prompted Samuel Champlain to name the island *l'Isle des Monts-déserts*, the island of barren mountains.

Boulder beaches are formed as the surf slowly turns these stones into rounded cobbles.

Harbor seals lounge on the shore at low tide. They are best seen on off-shore ledges which afford them protection from land predators and easier access to their fishing grounds.

Egg Rock Lighthouse, built in 1875, lights the entrance of Frenchman's Bay.
In the distance Schoodic Peninsula emerges from the fog.

If time permits, a trip to Schoodic Peninsula, about an hour's drive from Bar Harbor, should be part of your visit to Acadia. Schoodic Point feels the force of the ocean, often with dramatic displays. Mount Desert Island is in the distance.

The area's rich history can be found throughout the park in such places as Sieur de Monts Spring, the Abbe Museum of Indian antiquities, the Carroll Homestead in Southwest Harbor, and the Islesford Museum on Little Cranberry Island.

Acadia's geology is dramatically displayed on mountain summits and along its open shorelines. Pink granite is the major component of the island, but around the edges can be found evidence of the original bedrock and the upheaval it has experienced.

The park is littered with erratic boulders transported from miles away and left as the glacier retreated. Bubble Rock perched on the side of South Bubble Mountain has been here for twelve thousand years.

White-tailed deer and snowshoe hare are common browsers in the park.

The majestic bald eagle, the raucous pileated woodpecker and Maine's state bird, the chickadee, are just a few of the many birds commonly seen in Acadia.

A 50-mile carriage road system was built by John D. Rockefeller Jr. from 1913 to 1940, most of which was then donated to Acadia National Park. Designed for carriages, the roads are now also popular with runners, walkers, bicyclists and cross-country skiers.

This gatehouse at Jordan Pond and another in Northeast Harbor were built to house gatekeepers who would control carriage traffic onto the road system. The gatehouses were never actually used for that purpose and now house park employees.

The Cobblestone Bridge built in 1915 was the first of seventeen bridges that complement the carriage road system. This is the only bridge made from cobblestones which were meant to mirror the rounded stones in the streambed below.

The waterfall at Waterfall Bridge is best seen during the spring runoff or after a heavy rain. Because of the island's granite bedrock and shallow soil, waterfalls are often short-lived.

The carriage road system's intent was to provide access to the inner beauty of the island. It was designed using the natural contours of the land to minimize its impact and to maximize the view. Even the signs are intentionally vague giving a general direction but not a specific destination.

EAGLE LAKE
SEAL HARBOR
BUBBLE POND
N.E.HARBOR

PARADISE HILL
WITCH HOLE
HULLS COVE
DUCK BROOK

Bass Harbor Marsh is a tidal waterway meandering toward Western Mountain.

Nearly every pond in the park has a resident beaver population. The park's resource managers monitor beaver activity as it can conflict with the preservation of historical resources.

Bass Harbor Head Lighthouse is one of the most photographed lighthouses in the area and appears on the 2012 U.S. quarter.

Bear Island Lighthouse originally built in 1839 is best seen by boat. The current building, constructed in 1889, overlooks the passage to Northeast Harbor.

Rugosa rose brightens the shoreline in the early summer.

Baker Island, four miles off the coast of Mount Desert Island, was once home to a small farming community. Though the people are now gone, the view that they enjoyed remains.

Isle au Haut, another off-shore island further down the coast, is accessible by boat from Stonington. The island is a classic example of "the country of the pointed firs" with evergreen forests marching down to the sea. The island's geology, similar to that on Mount Desert Island, is dramatically exposed along its open shoreline.

Comparing Isle au Haut with Mount Desert Island one sees a significant difference. MDI's fall landscape marks the path of a devastating fire that swept across the island in 1947. Where the fire burned, evergreen forests have been replaced by colorful deciduous trees.

Along the Jesup Trail every season
has a unique character.

Cross country skiing, snowshoeing and ice fishing are but are few of the winter activities that keep local residents and hardy visitors entertained.

Winters in Acadia may be cold and long, but they bring a beauty that makes a visit worth the effort.

Bunchberry dogwood, sheep laurel and blue-flag iris are just a few of the spring flowers that are so welcomed after a long, white winter.

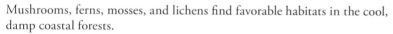

Mushrooms, ferns, mosses, and lichens find favorable habitats in the cool, damp coastal forests.

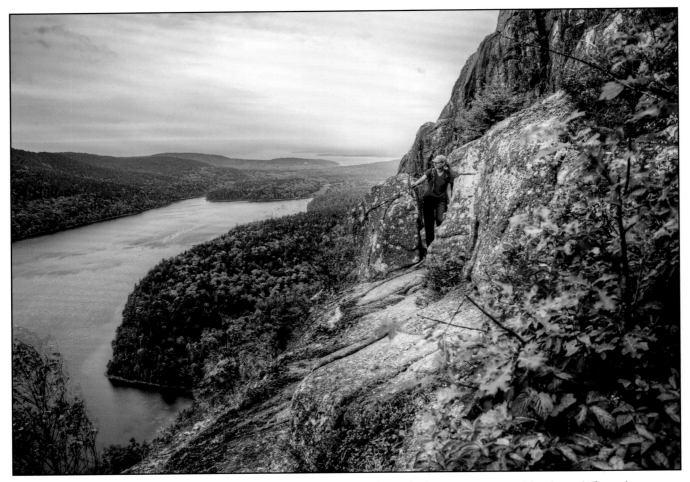

The contour of Acadia's mountains was shaped by the glaciers. Gentle north slopes are contrasted by sheer cliffs on the south-east. Today trails along these dramatic mountainsides are a favorite for hikers looking for a challenge.

One of the most dramatic and popular trails is the Precipice. The trail ascends to 1,058 feet in less than a mile. Scaling the face of Champlain Mountain is not for those with a fear of heights.

Acadia's experience extends far beyond its borders.
This view from Beech Mountain looks across
Long Pond to the mainland beyond.

Peace and tranquility can be found in the views from Acadia's open mountain summits.

The sunset may mark the end of daylight, but not the end of the day.

Acadia is one of the few places on the east coast with a clear view of the night sky. Seeing the Milky Way span across the landscape is a perfect way to end a day at Acadia National Park.